# GRANT WRITING
## what the pros know

*50 Things I Wish I Had Known Before Writing My First Grant*

Amanda Pearce, CFRE

Amanda Pearce, CFRE

www.fundingforgood.org


First printed May 2015.
Printed in the United States of America.

Disclaimer
Every effort has been made to accurately represent this product and its' potential. However, funding potential is dependent upon the person or persons using this material and the many circumstances surrounding a grant proposal submission.

Examples are not to be interpreted as a promise or guarantee of funding. The materials contained in this book are for informational purposes. I hope that the information presented here will help you be successful in fundraising, but no guarantees of return on investment or warranties are expressed or implied.

All links are for informational purposes only and are not warranted for content, accuracy or any other implied or explicit purpose.

ISBN: 978-0-692-45872-3

## Contents

# Foreword

One of the first things people think of when it comes to fundraising is grant writing.

After all, there are hundreds of foundations out there, and they exist for the sole purpose of giving away money to worthy charities, right?

While that's true, finding, writing, and getting grants is tricky business. There are lots of places where you can get off track or shoot yourself in the foot, and ruin your chances of winning a grant.

I know from my own experience that getting grants isn't easy. In fact, it took me nearly a year of hard work to get it right, and finally start generating a steady stream of fundraising revenue from grant writing. After that, I was able to consistently get grant money to fund operations, purchase equipment, start new programs, and hire staff.

When I met Mandy Pearce, I knew she was no ordinary grant master. She's found and received millions in grants. She's a wealth of knowledge and knows the subtle nuances that can make all the difference in being approved or denied.

Read this book. No, study this book. Apply what you read to your own work in grant writing. If you can learn to be half as good as Mandy, you'll be wildly successful in getting grants. – Sandy Rees, Get Fully Funded

## Question 1

What is the most important part of grant writing?

## 1. What is the most important part of grant writing?

Relationship Building. The most important part of all fundraising is relationship building. A key element in many development departments fundraising plans is grant writing. The key to *successful grant writing* is building solid relationships with foundations.

Depending on the foundation you are working with, you may be building a relationship with a program officer, secretary, 'gate-keeper', executive director or other staff person. Take this seriously. The person you are working with will likely be your voice to the people making decisions on grants awards. You want potential donors to know you, what you do, and what impact you can and do make. Most of all you want them to know you are sincere and there is a solid foundation to your relationship. Even if you don't get funded the first, or every time you apply, keep building the relationship. You never know where it will lead.

> ***I think that the most important part is attention to detail in the process, understanding what makes a philanthropic partner inclined to partner with your organization and being respectful of that relationship is crucial. Remember that you are writing to people, not just cold entities and they want you to tell them a story and demonstrate the impact of their investment in your partnership. Do your best to understand and anticipate their needs and where your relationship is headed, then capture that in your words. Also, words of gratitude are never lost on people.- Lynne M. Wester***

# Question 2

## How much should grant writers be paid?

2. **How much should grant writers be paid?**

This is a frequently asked question in the non-profit world, and honestly, the answer varies. Service rates directly reflect the work that is being completed.

- Are they writing proposals?
- Are they researching grants?
- Are they taking care of grant management (such as reporting and data collection)?
- Are they building the relationship with the potential donors?

There is a great deal grant writers could do, depending on the needs of an individual organization. You must first look closely at what you are doing, what you have time to do, and then what you are asking a grant writer to do for you. Rates will vary based on these variables, as well as individual experience level and history of success.

If you are working with a beginner grant writer who is seeking experience, obviously this person might not be able to charge as much as a seasoned professional.

Additionally, your location may pre-determine 'going rates' for grant writers. Websites exists specifically to provide average rates of occupations based on geographic location. These rates could be hourly or salaried. I recommend visiting such a site to compare salaries for grant writers in your area.

Commission-based versus fee-based grant writing is another topic that will likely come up in your conversation with professionals.

Many organizations exist to protect professionals in our field with a code of ethics.

The Association of Fundraising Professionals (AFP) is one such organization. As an AFP member myself, there is a code of ethics that I must abide by, which includes not working for commission. Some grant writers don't mind working and only being paid if an organization receives a grant. There are numerous issues with this practice.

1) If the proposal is not funded, the grant writer does not get compensated – even though they did the work.

2) Very few donors allow organizations to incorporate grant writer fees into the proposal budget. Therefore, it can seem a little unethical to pay a writer out of the grant funds, when grant writing services are not a budgeted line item.

3) The practice of commission based grant writing devalues the skill and experience many grant writers possess.

Consider the following analogy:

If you go to a doctor because you are sick, do you say, "I'm only going to pay you if you cure me"? No. We understand, as a society, that doctors' work is not an exact science. They may or may not be able to 'fix' you on-the-spot. But, no one would think of saying they weren't going to pay the office visit or fees associated with medicines that 'might' cure the problem, right? Why are grant writers often expected to write quality applications and not be paid for their work? No one has control over what a board decides concerning grant funding. Therefore, why should grant writers be held accountable if a grant is not funded?

Non-profit staff should educate themselves on the process of grant writing in order to review an application and determine if it has addressed the questions, answered them thoroughly, represented your program or project accurately and ultimately given you a quality product.

In short, there is no set amount grant writers *should* be paid. I encourage you to educate yourself and interview several potential candidates prior to making a final decision. In determining how much a grant writer should be paid, it is important to clarify services offered and associated fees.

# Question 3

## How do I build a relationship with a donor?

## 3. How do I build a relationship with a donor?

Relationship building is a skill that most of us learn through family and friends. Those skills are easily transferred to donors. It's really not as hard as everyone tries to make it. Relationship building is doing things for others that build a foundation of commonality, a base of things to discuss, knowledge of interests, and knowledge of the important things for the other person/organization.

In the non-profit world, there is the common practice of 7 donor touches every year. This means that non-profits should have 7 times a year they reach out and make contact or communicate with their donors. This does NOT mean making 7 asks. Perhaps 1-2 of these touches are asks, but saying 'thank-you' should occur much more often than asking for a gift.

Donor touches can be as simple as:

- A holiday greeting card
- An invitation to an event your organization is holding
- A tax letter at year's end
- A hand-written thank-you for a donation, continued support, volunteer time, committee work, recommendation for a board member, door being opened to another potential donor etc.
- An invitation to lunch or coffee just to catch up
- A personal phone call to update a donor on a campaign
- A personal invitation for a tour of a facility or program

These are just a few ideas for donor touches. As you get to know your donors individually, you will come up with amazing ways to reach out and make your touches even more personal.

Relationship building is just that… building. Any contractor would agree that a strong foundation is the first step in building a structurally sound home. The same concepts apply to building donor relations. You may not always get a call back or a response to an email, you may not get a yes to an invitation you sent or an acceptance for a lunch meeting… but the fact you offered, is a 'touch' and it is where you must start. You may not always start on a first-name basis and you may never get there… but truly… how long did it take you to become 'best friends' with your best friend? It didn't likely happen in an hour. You had to get to know each other, have experiences together, learn to communicate with each other… and show that you weren't going anywhere.

> ***Stop calling them funders. I would recommend partner or donor, but they don't simply fund us, it's a much more complex relationship. Funder implies it is a one way relationship and that we are not beholden to them, it also smacks of transactionality, not relationship. We need to really see these organizations as relationships, not just ATMs. They're people who care and gracious giving souls. Understand that what works for one partnership won't work for them all. Be respectful of their wishes and don't force yourself on them, as in all relationships trust and deep understanding takes time. Work together with them to help forward their mission and by extent your mission. One solution doesn't fit all here and we need to be respectful that people come together to make investments in our organizations and we can help them flourish and thrive as we do. Also don't forget the power and humility of hand written notes and communications with them that have nothing to do with the fact that you need something from them. – Lynne M. Wester***

## Question 4

## When should an organization start looking at grants?

**4. When should an organization start looking at grants?**

Would it surprise you to know that some non-profits have never, and will never turn to grant funding as part of their development plan? I have worked with non-profits that have been around over 50 years and are just now venturing into the grant world. They usually take the journey because of the economy, but not because they want to rely on grants. So, don't assume just because you are a non-profit organization, you are 'suppose' to apply for and rely on grants. That is not the case. Many experts in the field agree that a healthy non-profit should never depend on grant funding for more than 30% of its' total operating budget.

Consider the following when determining your organizations readiness to apply for grant:

1) If you are in a place where you have met your capacity (staff, space, program etc.), then it might be time to look at capacity building grants so you can grow.

2) If you have a capital campaign, you may consider making grants a portion of that campaign to ensure its' success and speedy completion.

3) If you are in a field where long term funding sources have been cut or eliminated, then you may need to look to grant funding until you can rework your game plan for sustainability.

4) If you have programs or projects that are excelling at what they do and you feel grants may highlight some of these opportunities and allow you to serve more in your field… perhaps it is time to research what is available in terms of grant dollars.

I also recommend considering this information.

1) You should never 'create' a program or project to fit a grant you have found. Decide on your needs, list them, understand them, and then research grants that match those needs.

2) If your organization has a budget or a previous year's budget in the 'red', you may not want to begin writing grants until you have a few years in the 'black'. Donors will see you as a risk and often times will not look favorably upon your request.

3) If your organization is in its' infancy, you may find seed money to support your work. Often donors require organizations to demonstrate their history of success prior to considering funding. In many cases donors may require 3-5 years of successful programming. So, despite a perfect fit on paper, you may not qualify due to the amount of time you have been providing services.

There are many nuances to consider before beginning to utilize grant writing as part of your annual fundraising plan. But, there is also a lot to consider each year before you decide to continue grant writing in your fundraising plan, or removing it, decreasing the dollars you hope to raise through grants, or reducing the dollars you need. Your reliance on grants should be strategic, and if need be, consult with peers or other development professionals to help analyze your individual organizational needs before making these changes.

# Question 5

## What type of funds should I look for?

## 5. What type of funds should I look for?

In order to know what types of funds to look for, you first need to know what your needs are. Once you list the program and projects for which you need support, you will then be able to make an accurate list of the types of funds for which you should be looking.

For example, let's say you have an office space and provide medical services in the community. If you currently have two doctors and two offices within your facility, but there is a daily waiting list of clients who are not seen, and other doctors willing to offer their services… perhaps you need a capacity building grant. You may need capacity building dollars to hire additional medical staff, move to a larger facility or rehab the current facility. Once the need is identified, it is easier to list the types of funds you may qualify to receive.

***Ones that will fund you. Nice answer, right? I have always felt that grant writing success is 90% research and 10% writing. Frankly, I have spent some time applying to foundations that said "only preselected charities can apply" when mine wasn't selected. I have used my considerable skills and my winning personality to the hilt, and I never succeeded!***

***If the mission and need of your agency doesn't match what a funder wants to fund, don't waste your time. When I teach individuals how to solicit gifts, I always tell them to go to your best prospect first. That means a person who is likely to say "yes". It means a person who loves the mission, has the capacity to make a gift, and the past history of being charitable. Seventy per cent of Americans are givers, and that means thirty per cent are not. Go with someone in the first group! The same concept is true with grants. Rank your prospects on mission synchronization, openness to be approached, and timing. Also be careful not to ask for too much. You can easily find out the past history of your prospect. If their largest historical grant is $100,000, don't ask for a million dollars. Ask for a little more than their lowest gift if it is a first-time ask.***

*I spent a year working on a huge project in mental health. I was asked to concentrate on private and corporate foundations rather than government grants. I learned a lot, much of it painful. Basically, the interest was not there to fund first-time grants for seven figures or over. It didn't work. And when I stepped out another firm came in and found the same thing. Every good idea is not fundable!*

*But your success will expand as you learn more about funders in general. Federal, state, foundation, and corporation funders have a dizzying range of opportunity. Explore them all as much as you can. But use your mission, gift range, and likelihood of success to figure out your best prospects. Then, go down them in sequence. – Alex Comfort, CFRE*

# What types of grant funding are out there?

## 6. What types of grant funding are out there?

There are numerous types of grant funding. Within various research software you will see many additional categories, but for general searching online, most programs and projects will fall into one of these categories. The following is a list I use frequently.

| | |
|---|---|
| Annual Campaigns | General / Operating Support |
| Building/Renovation | Internship Funds |
| Capital Campaigns | Land Acquisition |
| Conferences/Seminars | Matching / Challenge Support |
| Consulting Services | Project Grants |
| Continuing Support | Program Grants |
| Curriculum Development | Program-related Investment / Loans |
| Emergency Funds | Publication |
| Employee Matching Gifts | Research |
| Equipment | Scholarship Funds |
| Endowments | Seed Money |
| Exchange Programs | Technical Assistance |
| Fellowships | Travel |

# Question 7

## What are grant guidelines?

## 7. What are grant guidelines?

In short, grant guidelines are instructions. Grant guidelines are INSTRUCTIONS, not suggestions. Guidelines are a specific set of rules that an applicant should follow when developing a grant proposal.

Guidelines can be anywhere from one page, to hundreds of pages, depending on the agency/organization/foundation providing them. Typically, the larger the funding opportunity, the longer and more complex guidelines will be. Guidelines can include everything from font size and type to be used, to the spacing of the pages/margins, information to be included and left out, specific items to be addressed, how to submit the application etc. Additionally, state or federal grant guidelines will likely provide a breakdown of the scoring system to be utilized in the peer review process. The explanation of the scoring system will probably include point values for each question and if there are bonus points available. This is helpful as programs are designed and strengths and weaknesses are assessed.

**As I tell everyone I work with… read the guidelines, they are there for a reason. Before you begin writing one word on the application, read *every* word in the guidelines.**

Guidelines are a great way for donors to weed out applications. A funder will often discard an application based on lack of compliance with guidelines. While this may seem strict, it is only fair that a funder may assume if an applicant is unable to follow simple instructions in the guidelines, they may not comply with the grant contract if funded. This is a great reason to contact the program officer if you have questions or something is unclear. I have read hundreds of pages of guidelines for a grant that allowed a maximum of 40 pages to be submitted. Every page is important. Be thorough and know everything being requested before you begin writing.

# Question 8

## What is the difference between a local, state, and federal grant?

## 8. What is the difference between a local, state and federal grant?

A local grant is typically a grant that is only for a specific city, town, county, area. Hence the term 'local'. A grant from the US Department of Education for Tennessee would not be considered local, it would be a state grant.

Most local grants are going to be smaller in scale and the process for building a relationship with the donor and meeting with them is often easier.

Local grants often come from family foundations, community foundations, local corporate foundations, and private foundations.

State grants are often presented by departments, agencies or associations, like the Department of Education or Department of Agriculture, or statewide associations like a statewide Arts Councils. State grants can also include donors whose scope of service includes an entire state. In NC, Z. Smith Reynolds (ZSR) is a good example of a statewide donor. ZSR has specific priority areas, but will accept applications from qualifying agencies across the state.

Federal grant programs are created by Congress through the enactment of public laws and appropriation of funds. The disbursement follows a systematic progression based on publicly announced rules and is funded by public contributions, generally through annual legislative appropriations.

> Federal Appropriations are appropriated by Agencies & Departments:
> Examples of Agencies - NIH, NSF, NOAA, DARPA, NEH
> Examples of Departments - Defense, Energy, Education, EPA

Federal grants can be found on individual agency and department websites, as well as www.grants.gov.

## Question 9

## What should we do if we don't get funded?

## 9. What should we do if we don't get funded?

There is no guarantee a grant application will be selected for funding. An organization may have done all the right things, built a great relationship with the donor, submitted a fabulous proposal, and still not get funded. Why? It is important to note that program officers play a vital role in the grant writing process. However, they don't have the final say in who gets selected for funding. That is a board decision, a family decision if it's a family foundation which has say over the distribution, a random group of reviewer's scores that may determine the selected recipients etc. There is no way to know if a proposal will get funded prior to submitting an application.

You can educate yourself on the odds by asking how many applications were received, or how many are typically received… then asking how many applications are typically funded etc. But, you never know if you will get the dollars until you are notified.

If you don't get funded, you should do a few things.

1) Write a hand-written thank-you to the potential donor and thank them for considering your proposal. Let them know you appreciate the opportunity to be considered and look forward to applying in a future cycle.

2) Call the program officer and request feedback on what to do to strengthen your proposal in the future. You should also confirm that it would be okay to reapply during their next cycle.

3) Accept any feedback without arguing or making excuses. As hard as this can be, trust me, it is the only way to go. Arguing will not get you the dollars you applied for. It will only leave a bad impression with the potential donor. Be humble, say thank-you, and implement any changes they suggest.

4) If you are not encouraged to reapply… accept that feedback and mark them off your list for now, but keep the relationship building in place. You never know when you will have a project or program that peaks their interest in the future.

*A few years back I did some work with a struggling educational nonprofit. During my initial review of their past foundation support, I discovered on their list a foundation whose mission I thought aligned perfectly with this organization's mission, and also had a history of repeat funding. Yet, year after year, the foundation had declined this organization's proposals - even one year when they had specifically been invited to apply.*

*Frankly I didn't get it. It was tempting to put them in the "they'll never fund us pile" but I picked up the phone to call their executive director. Not knowing if I'd even reach a live person, I was delighted when he answered himself. I asked him rather bluntly why his foundation had not funded us. One month, one letter, and one site visit later the organization was the recipient of a $15,000 grant - the first of many.*

*It's always frustrating to have your grant proposal rejected, but it's absolutely essential to stay optimistic and to persevere. The fact is that most grant proposals do get rejected, but learning from the experience-examining why your proposal was turned down-- will benefit you by making future proposals stronger. And don't give up on one foundation because they have declined your proposal. Unless you specifically don't fall within their funding guidelines (in which case you probably shouldn't have wasted your time applying in the first place), you'll want to reapply as soon as you're able.*

*If you feel like you've done a solid job describing your non-profit's mission, the population you serve, and how your proposed grant would help your clients, then take another look at the foundation's mission.*

> *Did your proposal help the foundation meet its goals? Was it really a good fit in the first place?*

*Foundations routinely turn down the best conceived projects simply because the goals of the non-profit and the foundation aren't aligned. Explore the foundation's website, annual report and 990 to see what kind of projects they've funded in the past, and compare those projects to your own. See what you can learn, and if this step wasn't part of your last round of proposal applications, make it part of your next.*

*If you're confident that the goals of your proposal met the goals of the foundation, then go back to the original Request for Proposals. Evaluate the writing in your proposal. Consider the following questions:*

- *Did you state your needs clearly and specifically, right up front?*
- *Did you include information about your non-profit's other sources of funding to help show that you're a worthy cause?*
- *Did you use testimonials to bring the needs of your clients to life, and did you use meaningful, accurate data to support your organization's needs?*
- *Is your writing clear and compelling?*
- *Does the proposal sound like it's been written by one person, or do several different voices make it choppy and scattered?*
- *Is the formatting clean and consistent?*
- *Did you use headings and subheadings to make your proposal easily navigable?*

*If you've reevaluated your proposal and still have questions, call the foundation and ask to speak with the program officer who reviewed your proposal. After you've thanked them for their thoughtful review, ask:*

- *Is there anything we could have done differently in our proposal?*
- *May we resubmit for your next funding cycle?*
- *Are you aware of any other foundations that we might approach?*

*And always, always send a thank you note — even if you've been declined.*

*In your next round of grant proposals, build upon what you've learned. Send your applications to a diverse group of foundations, and be sure to explain how your project can help each foundation meets its own goals, not only how the foundation can help you meet yours. Above all-be patient, be persistent, and be positive. – Pamela Grow*

---

*Be as gracious. I think the interaction here should be no different than if you did get funded. You need to express to them that you would like a continued relationship and that you are willing to make investments in your organization to ensure that you become a partner in the future. Also be open to feedback and actively seek it out, ask why you didn't receive funding this time around and what you could do to ensure a better chance at success the next time. Listen to the feedback and thank them for it and then take action. Doing the same thing time and time again and expecting different results is the height of insanity. But above all else, be gracious and happy for the other organizations that did get funded. - Lynne M. Wester*

# Question 10

## What should we do if we do get funded?

## 10. What should we do if we do get funded?

Celebrate! If you get funded, you should be thankful you were chosen and express that appropriately to the donor.

Be sure that you know what forms of acknowledgement the donor is amenable to before you start sending out press releases, articles in the paper, e-blasts etc. Some donors are very intentional in asking for no recognition of their gifts. Make sure you respect these wishes. Other donors want all the recognition you can afford. Make every effort to know these things prior to being awarded funds so you can be on the ball when you are selected.

First and foremost, you need to pick up the phone and call the donor to say thank-you. You may speak to the program officer, the executive director or CEO, the owner of a company or a secretary. It really doesn't matter, as long as you say thank-you immediately. Make several calls if you have the contact information to do so, and be sincere.

Next, take out the stationary and ***hand write*** a thank you to the organization. Be original and show your gratitude in this correspondence. There is no need to write a book. Get that in the mail ASAP! Then proceed to recognize the organization in the manner in which they request, and the manner which is appropriate for the size of their gift.

Ideas for recognition will vary based on the gift amount, the donor wishes, and the resources at your disposal. Some ideas may include:

- Banner stands with customized appreciation wording
- Thank you lunch/coffee with donor
- Tour of the program/project 'in action' as dollars are used
- Press releases to local media
- Social media posts
- Story in your organizational newsletter
- Signage
- Bricks/tiles/walls of honor on construction projects
- Banners around a facility (sport fields, class rooms, etc.)

- Special presentation to the Foundation at a board meeting or annual meeting
- Presentation from a client/participant/beneficiary from the program/project at the Foundation's board meeting/annual meeting

The list is endless for ways you can recognize a donor. In order for you to have an impact on the donor, you need to get to know what *they* will appreciate. Not what *you think* they should appreciate, or what you would appreciate, but what *they* will appreciate.

I worked with an organization once that always wanted to spend a lot of money on donor gifts. The gifts chosen were generic items that truly had no meaning for the donors. Most donors don't want gifts and that's not why they give. Learn why the financial gifts are made before you plan the thank you efforts.

> ***What your organization should do if it gets funded is first and always thank the funder. Then schedule reports and updates as requested by the funder and any additional ones your organization might want to make.***
>
> ***ASK the funder if you can publicize the gift, and if so, how they want it publicized. They are now your partners not just your funders, so treat them like donor/partners.***
>
> ***Invite them to see their programs in action; send them thank you notes from service recipients; get out of the way and connect the funder with the beneficiary - just like you should every donor. – Annie Fritschner, ACFRE***

---

> ***The first thing you need to do once you've been funded is to send a warm, gracious thank you letter. Let the funder know the difference they're making with their gift. Make sure that you've included any information the funder has required — if the foundation has included a form requiring a signature, make sure you send it back (and they don't have to ask you twice).***

---

*When it comes to thanks, your letter will suffice. I recall how one organization we funded had an over-sized crystal plaque created. Total overkill.*

*Because I recommend a fairly heavy donor communications schedule, I don't typically recommend adding a funder to your organization's mailing list. What has worked well for me in the past has been to develop a 'foundation letter' highlighting key programs and organizational stories, and personalized for each funder. Send out one to three letters before the required grant reports.*

*And speaking of those required grant reports: get them in, and get them in on-time. If you've been given a format to follow, follow it to the letter. Tie it back to your original grant proposal and efficiently demonstrate that you did what you said you'd do.*

*What if things didn't quite work out as planned? That pilot program only ended up serving half the number of clients you had planned for? Never hedge or make excuses. Your transparency will be valued. Be matter of fact and straightforward about what went wrong, and what steps you've taken to rectify it.*
*– Pamela Grow*

---

*Again, graciousness is key here. Follow up and transparency are essential for your success. Ensure that you are following their process every step of the way and meet or beat their deadlines. Hand written notes are always a great idea. Put measures in place to ensure that the money will be spent according to the intent of the grant and that you can proactively report its' progress along the way. The more proactive you are, the more likely you are to get funded again the next time. Waiting until the end to report on your activities is far too late.*
*– Lynne M. Wester*

## Question 11

Can we apply to more than one potential donor for the same program or project?

**11. Can we apply to more than one potential donor for the same program or project?**

Of course! As long as you are honest in your representation of what you need and up front when donor asks who you are soliciting to support your program/project, there is no reason why you can't go to multiple donors. In fact, a lot of donors *want* to know you have solicited numerous supporters for your cause.

Why, you ask? Well, if a donor knows that you have solicited several Organizations and/or individuals for support and perhaps you have some proposals out there that are pending approval, some have been approved, some have been declined and you have money in hand for others… then they know their dollars are not the *only* dollars that will make or break your ability to move forward.

A lot of people I talk to are very hesitant to share the list of folks they are asking, or have asked for support, because they think it will deter potential donors from selecting their organization for support. If you build a good relationship with a donor, you will know what they are looking for and why they are asking those types of questions. Think about this as well; if one foundation sees you have support from other foundations or individuals, they are more likely to think your project has merit if others are willing to invest in it.

It is important to be up front with donors in another way. If you receive excess funding for a project because you have solicited multiple prospects, you need to reach out to the donors who 'put you over your goal' and explain what has happened. A great line I like to use is this:

> ***"Thank you so much for selecting our program/project for funding. I wanted to reach out to you and let you know that we have been very blessed and have received more funding that we initially requested. Your dollars are very much appreciated and I would like to ask if it might be possible to use these funds towards …. (here you need to fill in the blank with an addition to your project, add dollars to line items that already exist, offer another project, etc.) which we could also***

***very much use at this time. We would be happy to revise the original proposal for your records if this might be a possibility."***

Keep in mind that the foundation may say no, and in that case you would need to return the funding. I rarely see foundations request their money back in these cases, but it does happen. If you have built the strong relationship with the donor that you should have, this will likely be a fairly painless conversation. Be upfront and honest. It would be unethical to use those dollars for anything other than the way outlined in the grant without approval from the foundation or individual beforehand.

> ***Yes. Seeking a grant is like seeking a business loan, in that a grant is a social investment—most funders do not want to shoulder the risk of the entire enterprise failing. Funders want to see that other, reputable grant makers are supporting your organization, or that you are planning to approach other grant makers that might support your project. They want to see that you are savvy and that you will be able to sustain any efforts that receive grants. Of course, you can't "double dip"—you can't accept two $20,000 grants for the same $20,000 expense. If the grants you receive add up to more than what you need, which rarely happens, you can always speak with one of the funders and ask to re-purpose the funds or simply return them. – Mark Goldstein, CFRE***

# Question 12

# What is a LOI?

## 12. What is a LOI?

There are two specific items associated with the abbreviation LOI. It is important to know which you are being asked to provide.

**Letter of Inquiry -** When an organization requests a Letter of Inquiry from you, they are asking you to compose a letter, most of which will include the same information as your executive summary, and *inquire*, if you could submit a grant application. Basically, does your proposal fit the priorities of the foundation, is it something they either have funded in the past, or might be likely to fund now, do they feel your idea is fully developed, is the amount you are asking for something they would consider and so on.

**Letter of Intent** - When an organization requests a Letter of Intent, they are asking you to let them know you are going to apply. Again, you will include the same information from your executive summary (who you are, what you do, what your need is, how much you are asking them to support and what you hope to do with the funds should you be chosen to receive a grant), and then let them know during which cycle you *intend* to apply.

The main difference here is that with one you are asking for permission, and with the other you are informing them of your intentions. With a Letter of Intent it is still possible for a foundation to contact you for further information or to advise you based on the information you provided.

# Question 13

# What is a RFP or CFP?

### 13. What is a RFP or CFP?

In the non-profit world, Request for Proposals (RFPs) or Call for Proposals (CFPs) are solicitations made by an agencies, departments or foundations for entities that may be interested in submitting grant proposals ( in the for-profit world, often these are solicitations for bids on work contracts). Often time we see these terms used on www.grants.gov and via major funding foundations. Smaller foundations and corporations typically use the following terms interchangeably: grant proposals, applications or requests for funding.

# Question 14

What are the main parts of a grant proposal?

## 14. What are the main parts of a grant proposal?

There are 7 main elements to most grants proposals. There will be some proposals that won't utilize all of these and some that will have more, some that use the same concepts with different titles and some that just ask you broad, general questions. But, for the majority of donors, they want to see the following:

1) Title
2) Executive Summary
3) Organizational Information
4) Statement of Need
5) Project Description
6) Budget
7) Evaluation Method

# Question 15

# What makes a good title?

## 15. What makes a good title?

A good title is something that entices the reader to learn more. I like to use the example of the movie, The Sixth Sense. Well, we all know there are 5 senses… but what in the world is the 6th?! Everyone wanted to learn more. You need to do the same with your titles. As someone who has reviewed grants before, I can attest to the fact that titles are very important! A title will capture someone's attention, even briefly, and it will also stand out in their mind as they sift through piles of really horrible titles. I have seen titles like 'Basketball Court', 'Safety Seats for Kids', 'Mammograms', etc. These titles sure tell you what the grant is about, but not in a creative or inventive way. Put yourself in the readers' seat… what would you need to see to capture your interest?

# Question 16

## What should be included in the Executive Summary?

## 16. What should be included in the Executive Summary?

The executive summary is just that, a summary. You need to make sure that all of your pieces are coherent and persuasive because this is the foundation for the rest of your proposal.

You will want to describe the problem you are having. If you didn't have a problem, be it shortage of funds, more space, more staff, program expansion etc., then you wouldn't be looking for grant funding.

You need to include a few key descriptors of the program or project for which you are requesting support.

Next you should state what makes your program extraordinary and how your organization is uniquely positioned. These are two VERY different statements.

Here is a sample executive summary that outlines each of these areas very succinctly.

**Sample Executive Summary:**

Centro Hispano provides a humanitarian response to the critical needs of the Latino community in Western NC. We are writing to request $25,000 as salary support for tutors of our after school program, High Achievers (HA). HA is currently the only afterschool program in this region that specifically serves the 2,538 Hispanic students enrolled in our schools.

HA was designed in 2004 to help students and families bridge the social and cultural barriers that can have a negative impact on students' academic achievement. Since its inception the program has expanded from 40 to 205 students. Due to increased enrollment we have a need for additional tutors but lack funding to provide them. HA strives to meet the academic, social, and cultural needs of Hispanic families in our community through tutoring, cultural enrichment activities, teambuilding, leadership events, and a focus on prevention of risky behavior.

---

Last year, elementary students in HA achieved an average increase of 10.53 in reading skills and 8.35 in math skills among students tracked. In 2004-2005 only 68% of the region's schools met the Adequate Yearly Progress Requirements. School officials believe the significant increase of Hispanic students with limited English proficiency played a major role in the county's low test scores because state tests were designed based on the assumption of semi-fluency in the English language.

As HA enrollment continues to grow, please consider assisting us so we may hire additional tutors to serve more students effectively.

***It's important to be clear about why your organization needs this now. A sense of importance and urgency is necessary to get people to take action.***

***Be sure to share how this support will help your cause. Tell a story and remember that as an organization it is your role to facilitate change that is important to others.***

***People are not interested in funding your existence they are interested in funding your impact. – Beth Brodovsky***

## Question 17

What type of organizational information should we include/not include?

## 17. What type of organizational information should we include/not include?

Organizational information should be incorporated into the text of your proposal and should include the following:

- Official name of the organization, in addition to any nickname or acronym you plan to refer to during the proposal
- Organizational mission and/or vision statement
- A ***brief*** history of the organization
- Major program and/or primary activities of the organization
- Links with similar organizations
- Awards and/or accreditations
- Collaborations
- Number and capacity of staff

**Sample Organizational Information #1:**

Safe Harbor Rescue Mission was established in November 2004 to begin offering resources to a population of women in Catawba County that had no other support.

Safe Harbor has grown from one part-time staff and five clients in 2004, to 11 staff, an ever increasing number of volunteers and over 250 clients annually in 2011. As a non-profit, the ministry Safe Harbor brought to this area served needs of women in a unique way that created community support and eventually, great success. The ministries offered here are grace-based, Christ-centered assistance programs. Women are being served who are homeless, abused, addicted, abandoned and those simply defined as having a lack of resources.

Safe Harbor has become known as a place with many faces in our community. Safe Harbor serves over 250 women and children annually, and touches lives throughout our community in ways that cannot be measured in numbers. While our ministries would love to see the need for services diminish over time, which is rarely the case. In the current economic climate, the need for our programming has only increased. Unemployment rates in NC in September 2011 were 10% and in Catawba County those numbers rose to 11.9%, propelling us to 8th in the nation for unemployment. Families seeking food and nutrition assistance rose 389% between 2000 and June 2010 and 44.6% of Food Assistance recipients in 2010 were 20 years of age or younger.

The ladies served at Safe Harbor are often time unemployed, suffering from addiction or recovery, have been in or are in abusive situations, homeless and suffering from mental illness. Any one of these issues would be enough to overwhelm the majority of people, and at Safe Harbor we try to offer support, counseling, programming and stability to assist these women in putting their lives back in a manageable place.

**Sample Organizational Information #2:**

Since its inception in August 1999, Centro Hispano (CH) has grown, expanded and become the face of the Latino community for WNC County. We currently touch over 8,000 lives annually through our office and that number is constantly increasing. Our director, is the integral cog that holds the machinery of CH together and through her guidance, CH has been able to successfully work within the community at large to encourage Latino acculturation and acceptance.

The responsibilities at CH are ever increasing and currently cover such areas as: interpretation services for everything from court services, immigration questions, making doctor appointments, teaching classes in the community for expectant parents, offering assistance to those involved with DSS, etc. Parenting classes, DWI/Drug classes, serving as a school liaison for parents with little to no grasp of the English language, as well as presenter to school administrators to assist in closing the cultural gap in our community, teaching pre-natal classes, organizing community/cultural events, immigration clinics, 'Abriendo Puertas' after-school program, health forums and clinics (i.e. free mammograms, prostrate exams, breast cancer presentations, diabetes discussions, etc.)

This is, by far, not a complete list of services offer at CH, because the community needs are constantly growing and changing. Our services reach the entire community and we continually reshape our goals and services to reflect what the Latino community requests and exhibits in need. We enjoy participating in all areas of acculturation in the Latino community. Our focus here at CH is imperative to the continued partnerships of Latinos and non-Latinos in WNC County. In order to continue offering needed services, we rely on organizations such as H.I.P to assist us as we continue to develop as an organization and offer better, more efficient services to our clients and community.

# Question 18

## How do I develop a statement of need?

## 18. How do I develop a statement of need?

The building blocks of a strong statement of need are why, who and supportive data and/or statistics.

Explain why this project is necessary. Describe the nature of the problem – the nagging research question, the difficulties people face, etc. Much like researching – think broad first, and then narrow. Start with the generalized problem as it exists/occurs in your community. Then explain the conditions which make this a problem.

If there are others addressing the problem, identify gaps in what they're doing – and how you're project will fill those gaps. Be cautious not to be critical. As you investigate the need for specific programs within your community, it is imperative to avoid duplication of services. Where services may overlap, consider strategic collaborations.

- Let the donor know that you fully understand the problem at all levels.
- Use statistics to support your case.
- Use extreme adjectives (inadequate, outdated, tiny, underserved,etc.)
- Use graphics and be clear and concise
- Use factual, objective, well-supported, current information to substantiate the need for your program (authorities in the field as well as from your organization's own experience)
- Strike a balance between 'need' and 'hopelessness'
- Don't editorialize
- Avoid negativity

I like to answer the following questions when developing a statement of need.

1) What is the need or problem?
2) Who has the need or problem?
3) Why is this a need or problem?
4) What will happen if the need or problem is not addressed?
5) How do you know this information?

---

*All non-profits are organized to provide a service. It is imperative to be able to state this service quickly and in a compelling way. The "elevator speech" concept was conceived as a way to allow a board member or volunteer to explain the need to someone in the time it takes to go up 25 seconds in an elevator to someone. At a university I served we had a special emphasis on the liberal arts and how it prepared students to think conceptually. We finally started to say: "The world is getting more complicated and we teach students how to think. They come out able to conceive the future, pivot nimbly when necessary, and stay one step ahead of what changes."*

*Hopefully, the Mission Statement gives you a place to begin. If not, the key staff members should be able to explain the need in a cogent way. Past brochures for the annual campaign are other places to look. But there is a key: your need statement must be connected to emotion as much as possible. All funders, whether they be foundations, corporations, or even government agencies, are made up of people who sit around a table and discuss what the value of the grant is, what it achieves. When I consult with arts organizations these days, I tell them to focus on how our lives are enriched by what they do.*

*But remember, your value is best understood when it can be measured. One of my current clients is a relatively small hospital. We talk about how many people it serves, the impressive credentials of its physicians, how the numbers of patients in particular departments (like cancer) is increasing, and how it conserves costs. All are listed with numbers. But we also reference the awards it wins (seventh nationally in being the safest hospital in the country).*

*Ultimately, however, all development officers are story tellers. Your need statement must move the people listening to believe in your mission. One of my current clients is a small non-profit taking at risk students and teaching them leadership by putting them in a variety of summer camp settings. They have had amazing success, but they were trying to raise money without telling stories of success. Their need statement is now much better by use of real stories of young people who have succeeded because of their efforts. However, grants tell stories in a different way than I do sitting with a major donor. Make sure any stories are generalized to work with your narrative. And remember that a grant needs to emphasize impact, numbers, and measurability.*

*Finally, know your audience! Your need statement should focus on what your potential funder wants. The Request For Proposal (RFP) or foundation information will tell you a lot. When in doubt, call them up and see what they will tell you on the phone – don't overdo it but get to know them and allow them to get to know you. And if it is a corporation or corporate foundation, don't miss the fact that they are a business and it would be great if you could enhance their marketing by giving you a grant.*

*If your need statement is concise, emotional, measurable, and based on compelling stories of how you have impacted people in need, you stand a good chance of getting funded. – Alex Comfort, CFRE*

---

*A statement of need is better known as a case statement, and there are two types of case statements; there is the internal case statement which is developed by many people and managed by one person, or written by one person with lots if assistance; and there is the external case which is the pretty, edited version for the public.*

*The internal case is a document of any length (as long as it needs to be) clearly stating the organization's needs, strengths, weaknesses, vision, goals and all budgetary information per program. Sometimes organizations like hospitals or colleges will ask each department head to write their own statement with the same criteria to be included in it; sometimes smaller organizations will ask one person to interview the program managers and write the document so that the voice is consistent and the information gathered is similar.*

*But this document is for a very few eyes only because it is brutally honest and the language is clear and direct.*

*What the public and funders see is a document which has been dramatically edited, with attractive photographs, laid out in a professional manner, and which is much shorter. It lays out the*

***needs through first person statements, photographs, and a variety of messaging techniques.***

***Developing the internal case which is the baseline for the external case includes questions such as:***

- ***What is the value of our organization?***
- ***Should we still be in business and why?***
- ***Where are our unique services and where are certain services replicated or duplicated?***
- ***And if there are duplications, why should we still be providing that service?***
- ***What markets are being underserved? Are these the areas in which we want to expand?***
- ***How can we go out of business?***

***List all the questions and answer them by many stakeholders so that there can be a vigorous discussion. – Annie Fritschner, ACFRE***

I have provided two sample statements of need and one needs assessment for comparison. The difference being that a needs assessment usually requires more quantified data and statistics to support a need. A clear difference in style can been seen between the first two samples and the last.

**Sample Statement of Need #1:**

This request is for $25,000 general operating expenses, will be partially applied to salaries, toward an official audit and a bilingual website. We incur approximately $95,000 annually in general expenses (these costs are not covered by specific program grants, such as the NC-DSS grant). These expenses include the salaries and benefits for our Executive Director, Administrative Assistant and child-care providers, office rent, supplies, insurances and any other projects we hope to accomplish (i.e. audit/website).

Our Executive Director (ED) is a Hispanic who has led the organization since its founding in 1999, and is vital to leading our organization and connecting with our social service network and other Hispanic help agencies. She is well known and respected throughout the Hispanic and non-Hispanic communities, both locally and state-wide. The bilingual Administrative Assistant (AA) works directly with local agencies, those who come to our organization for help, and those who phone for assistance. In essence, she is our face to the community with whom we work. She is familiar with our computer programs and experienced in record keeping requirements. The AA is involved in every aspect of programming from translation services, notary services, pregnancy testing, teaching computer classes and the daily assisting of clients.

Although we have received general operating grant funding from other foundations of $5,000 to $40,000 each year toward our $95,000 requirement, these receipts have been irregular and uncertain. Other general expense funding comes from local churches, individual donors, local businesses and client "donations" for services rendered. Fluctuation of donations from these unreliable sources threatens the core of our service base, our staff. Despite the fund raising efforts of the staff and the organization's Board of Directors, every year has been a struggle to obtain sustainable funding for general operating expenses.

A grant of $25,000 from No Name Bank will help maintain the employment of our talented and dedicated staff, which in turn will enable our numerous programs in the areas of health, human services, education and arts and culture to continue to benefit the increasing local Hispanic population. By having an audit we will become eligible to apply for numerous grants that are not currently available to us. In addition we will broaden the scope of our service with a bilingual website, become more accessible to those unable to come in for information/services, and show future investors that we are trying to offer clients the most up-to-date services

**Sample Statement of Need #2:**

The Hispanic population increased by 1,050% in WNC County between the years 1990 and 2000. Currently, approximately 15,000-20,000 Latinos call our community "home" and are becoming active members of our society. The schools and other educational resources are not fully equipped financially, culturally, and or time-wise to serve such a large minority population, and are constantly turning to Centro Hispano (CH) as their primary resource.

Our local public schools received a letter in January stating test scores were extremely low and all resources should be directed to better train teachers to meet the educational needs of the ESL students. Centro Hispano's program, "Abriendo Puertas," is playing a vital role in this process. Not only do participants in the program receive an advocate who will interpret for parent/teacher conferences, they also receive assistance with homework, workshops on life skills, enrichment and prevention activities. Within a two week period last school year, concerned parents brought five young teenagers to CH, "drugged up and beat up" after a gang initiation process. The gangs have come to our community and many of the Hispanic youth are getting arrested for drug and gang related activities.

"Abriendo Puertas" is the only program in our region of WNC actively addressing these issues at such a large scale. Our partnerships with the Police Department, Juvenile Justice, Rape Crisis Center, YMCA, and other valuable community agencies enhance our ability to serve these young Hispanics and insure that high school graduation and careers take priority in their lives.

The summer programming of "Abriendo Puertas" is designed to provide healthy alternatives for youth and adolescents who might otherwise become involved in risky behavior such drug and alcohol use, gangs, teen pregnancy, and violence. Health education and fitness will be instruments used to promote mental, physical, and emotional health.

**Needs Assessment (for a state grant) #3:**

WNC County, population approximately 142,000 covering 400 sq. miles saw an increase of *1050%* in its Latino population between 1990 and 2000. The state increase rose 450% over the same period. Currently there are at least 8,000 Latinos living in WNC County according to the 2000 Census. There are approximately 14,000 Latinos living in the border counties of WNC#2, WNC#3, WNC#4, and WNC#5. This figure does not include the many Latinos that went unreported on the Census due to lack of understanding of the information or to undocumented adults declining to answer census questions. Hispanics are the ethnic group with the largest growth population in the county, and compose 27% of the population. In the last four years, the Latino population in WNC County increased by 15%.

In 2004, 17% of all teen pregnancies in WNC County were to Hispanic teens ages 15-19. In the US, half of Latinas have sexual intercourse before age 16. The Child Welfare League of America says that Latino teens becoming pregnant are more likely than their white or black counterparts to have dropped out of school prior to becoming pregnant and are less likely to return to school after the birth of the child. They also report that Latino children receive less sex information from their parents than non-Latinos. CH's Abriendo Puertas will specifically offer the Children First's programs addressing issues around early pregnancy, including poverty prevention, drug, alcohol, and violence prevention in addition to the sexuality and HIV/AIDS components.

Additionally, the current level of educational attainment among all workers 25 and older in WNC County's Metropolitan Statistical Area *is the lowest in NC's 11 MSA's* in percentage of high school and college graduates. Dropout information for the 2004-2005 school year indicates a slightly higher percentage of Hispanics (9.3%) than Caucasians (6.7%) dropping out. According to a 2003 WNC County Community Assessment Survey, 78.9% of survey respondents rated the growth in the Hispanic population over the last 10 years to be a very serious issue in the community. Of those, 77% stated that they that the issue was being addressed "inadequately."

Language and reading proficiency is a critical issue for Latinos. Language, service use, and transportation barriers are clearly affecting the well-being of children in these families– health, educational, social, and career development for Latino children is far behind that of their English-speaking counterparts. Latino children ages 0-17 make up 6.7 % or 2,305 of WNC County's Latino reported population.

School enrollment of Latino students in school year 2,004- 2005 school year was approximately 1,150. During 2002-2003, Latino competency scores in reading and math for middle school students were 53-74% compared to 81-89% for whites. High school end of course competency for Latino students during the same year were 46-67% compared to 76-85% of whites. The 2005 Adequate Yearly Progress Results for WNC County indicated that only 19.6 % of Hispanic 10$^{th}$ graders tested at or above grade level in reading. However, in mathematics, 79.5% of the same students tested at or above grade level.

Currently, there are approximately 150 students registered in the Abriendo Puertas program and of those approximately 100 are being serviced regularly. Last year, elementary students in the program achieved an average increase of 10.53 points in reading skills and 8.35 points in math skills in the students tracked. In 2004-2005 only 68% of the county's schools met the Adequate Yearly Progress Requirements. School officials believe that the significant increase of Hispanic students with limited English proficiency played a major role in the county's low test scores due to the fact that state tests were designed based on the assumption of semi fluency in the English language because tests were designed based on the assumption of semi fluency in the English language.

In addition to concerns over academic performance and the high drop our rate of Hispanic students, our once quiet community is now being faced with the reality of drugs, alcohol, and gang activity. Within the last two weeks, five families have come to CH seeking help for their 15-18 years old children who have come home drugged up, beat up, and with no memory of what happened to them during the party or gang initiation process.

One 15 year old Latina was dropped in front of her house at 3:00am with a large sum of money in her purse. Another 15-year old victim of the same social group claims that if she tells anyone who she is with or what they have done, they will kill her.

WNC County recently hosted a peaceful gathering of more than 500 Latinos who want American citizens to recognize immigrants who desire unity, freedom, and the opportunity to pursue the American dream. As CH staff members were leaving this event, five young men ages 15-17 began to ask questions about the *Abriendo Puertas* prevention class for teens (with prompting from an older and concerned sibling). All agreed to seek help for their drug and alcohol abuse under the condition that they could invite their friends and that the program would sponsor "some fun activities."

This program truly is opening the doors to life and education of a generation of young people who have fallen prey to the gang activity in WNC County Schools. The *Abriendo Puertas* program is working first-hand with the Police Department anti-gang task force, mental health providers, the Department of Juvenile Justice, and America's Addiction Treatment Center in order to offer prevention classes for these young Latinos. This year, a local mental health agency agreed to service 8 of our program participants at no charge as a show of support for the after-school program and as a gift to these young people. *Abriendo Puertas* and her community partners recognize the great need for our community to take a stand against drugs, alcohol, and violence. It is with this vision in mind that Centro Hispano requests consideration for funding in the amount of $125,000.

# Question 19

What does a project description include?

## 19. What does a project description include?

A quality project description should address the following:

- What is going to be done?
- Why does it need to be done?
- Who is going to benefit?
- How are you going to do it?
- How much will it cost?
- Where and when will the program/project take place?
- Who is going to do the work?
- What are their credentials?
- What are the program and/or organization credentials?

Once you have an answer to each of these questions, compile them in a concise narrative. This will become your project narrative, and if done well, should answer the majority of a donor's questions regarding your project.

**Sample Project Description #1:**

Outlaw Pottery would like to offer summer pottery programming for youth with special needs, specifically youth attending the All Children Together (ACT) program, to enhance their mental and emotional well-being, offer them new opportunities to explore their own interests, and provide them with hand-on arts classes since they are unable to experience art classes during the school year.

"According to the Surgeon General's report on mental health, released in December 1999, 22-23% of American adults, 44 million people – have diagnosable mental disorders. Based on these estimates, more than 1.5 million North Carolinians have mental illness. About 680,000 of them experience some functional impairment because of their illness." The US Surgeon General also reports 1 of every 10 children and adolescents has a diagnosable emotional or mental illness that warrants intervention. Five percent experience extreme impairment – what is called Serious Emotional Disorders, or SED's.

In the 1940's, artists working in psychiatric hospitals became aware that painting, drawing and other forms of artwork could form the basis of a therapeutic relationship between patient and therapist. The patients' creations are said to reveal hidden feelings and emotions and so help the therapist to better understand the patient as well as being an important medium for communication. Art Therapy is the creative use of paint, pastels, clay or art materials to help people communicate and overcome emotional and mental problems. Art is a powerful form of self-expression and is now considered to be a valuable therapeutic tool.

This 6 week class will offer an array of pottery projects, sculpting and Raku experiences for youth. The location of the pottery studio in The Newton Destination for the Arts will offer an ideal setting for the youth of ACT as their building is located directly next door. ACT serves youth from all over WNC County with behavioral and emotional challenges, so this project has the potential to have wide reaching effects. Since ACT has programming year-round, we found summer a great time to introduce art programming to see how it might fit in to the school year schedule and evaluate the success of the program.

The summer program will consist of 6 class sessions with a classroom of students from ACT, Outlaw Potter's Jason and Rosalie as Instructors, a local professional, who has worked for years with behaviorally challenged youth and has a master's degree in Special Education serving as assistant, and the Founder of The Heart of Virginia Foundation, Music for Mental Health and College Corps as assistant. These structured classes will offer projects for youth to explore their personal interests express themselves artistically and experience new ideas through various mediums. Students will have 4 to 6 pieces of glazed and fired pottery to take home at the end of their 6 weeks and hopefully wonderful stories to share with their families and friends.

For this summer program our local mental health agency has agreed to provide the cash to transport the students by van, pay for staff hours to transport, and pay for a staff to go with the students to class, as well as put in up to $100.00 for materials. (Staff to drive and monitor vans $10.99 per hour. 2 staff, roughly 2 hours daily time, 6 weeks=$275.00 and van rental $56.00 daily plus gas)

The Newton Destination for the Arts has graciously offered to let us use the space for 3 hours per class (1 hour of prep time, 1 hour of class and 1 hour to process the pieces after youth leave, firing the kilns, etc.) at a rate of $50/class.

We hope to use our art form as a tool to open up the world of possibilities for these youth. With a successful summer program we hope to explore the possibilities of an art program to serve the youth of WNC County, home schoolers and other youth with special needs during the school year. With the limited number of program opportunities for youth with special needs in our area, we hope you will partner with us to create some unique opportunities for those in our area. Thank you for the opportunity to present our proposal to you and we look forward to hearing from you soon.

**Sample Project Description #2:**

Lift Every Voice Project Description

Piedmont Percussion Program would like to request $3,500 from The Supporting Foundation to conduct a talent search, by audition, in our inner city and/or lower income/lower opportunity communities, focusing primarily on minority "at risk" teens between the ages of 13 and 18. We conducted a similar program called "Real Deal" in 2007 which was hugely successful and is still talked about. Numerous youth who excelled in the 2007 project have gone on to begin professional music careers and fulfill many of their personal goals and dreams as a result of their involvement in "Real Deal". "Life Every Voice" will concentrate on the talent in the gospel arena and is presented here in four stages.

**1.** An announcement will go out to all WNC County communities that a talent search will take place, date TBA, location: Ridgeplace Center. The talent will be concentrated in the area of gospel vocalists. The panel of judges will include musicians and educators from our area in an "American Idol" format. A total of 7-8 finalists will be chosen to go onto the next stage. Those who audition but are not chosen finalist, will be asked to join us as the "choir" for the last phase of the project.

**2.** Along with several assistants, a recording engineer, and musicians, I will help professionally "record" and accompany the musical finalists in multiple sessions at a professional recording studio. Each musician will be coached, rehearsed and guided along the tedious process of recording by trained gospel musicians from the Chartown area.

**3**. Upon completion of the artwork for the CD cover, 1000 CDs will be duplicated. The CD's will then be distributed for free. The names of all the semi-finalists as well as credits to all those involved, (including Grant funding) will be included on the CD. The CD will be given to local radio stations for guaranteed air-time. Mp3's and J-pegs will be posted on a website for free download.

**4**. A community concert with a guest speaker will take place to promote and celebrate all those chosen at either the Ridgeplace Center or First United Methodist Church of WNC County. The same musicians that recorded on the CD will perform with the youth, along with the choir of finalists and semifinalists. The concert will be free and open to the public, and CDs will be distributed for free at the concert to every person that attends. The 2007 community concert for "Real Deal" had over 1,000 attendees. It was an amazing turnout and community event.

This proposal aims to strengthen our community through by giving our at-risk teens a sense of purpose, accomplishment, direction, and above all, a necessary form of self-expression, as well as an opportunity to show their peers, families, and community the talent that exists within them. In most circumstances, these youth would never have this type of opportunity.

# Question 20

## Do I create my own budget?

## 20. Do I create my own budget?

Each grant application will have a unique set of guidelines. The budget will be one of the items addressed in the guidelines. Some donors will want you to use a standardized budget form, which they will provide for you, and others will want you to create a simple budget yourself. Reading the grant guidelines carefully will make budget expectations clear.

If you are completing an online application you may have a form to fill out, or you may need to upload a budget form (provided or created) into the online system. Again, reading through the application online beforehand will save you time and energy as you prepare your budget.

When a budget form is provided, the line items may or may not align with the ones you have created. You will need to rework your line items to fit into the categories provided. Often times there is a line labeled "Other". This line will contain anything that does not neatly fit into one of the other categories. Make sure you remember how you 'reallocated' your line items and what all you have included on each line. I often find it helpful to create a budget with what comprises each line item and print it out to keep with my hard copy files in case questions come up later.

A well prepared budget justifies all expenses and is consistent with the project description. Basic components and parameters to consider when creating a budget are:

- Duration
- How much are you asking the donor to support
- Level and resource commitment from your organization
- Number/identity/level of commitment of collaborating organizations
- Detail commitments of partners
- Keep it simple but be specific
- Create reasonable forecasts
- Be consistent with your budget, even if you submit numerous proposals

# Question 21

# What are evaluation methods?

## 21. What are evaluation methods?

Evaluation methods are the criteria for evaluating the success of a program or project. This tells the donor that you want to know if you've achieved your goals and objectives.

An evaluation plan tells many things.

- How you will know (the criteria you will use to evaluate success – tests, surveys, etc.)
- Methods that will be used to collect evaluation information
- Methods that will be used to analyze the evaluation information
- When you will conduct the evaluations (milestones, quarterly, annually)
- Describes who is going to evaluate (qualifications, credentials)

Evaluation is about being open to continuing feedback and adjusting your program(s) accordingly.

The three main types of evaluation methods are goal based, process based and outcomes based. Goal based evaluations measure if objectives have been achieved. Process based evaluations analyze strengths and weaknesses. Outcomes based evaluations examine broader impacts and often investigate what greater good was served as a result of the program or project.

Some things to consider when selecting an evaluation method are:

- What information is needed to make decisions?
- What information can feasibly be collected and analyzed?
- How accurate will the information be?
- Will the information be credible to top donors or management?

**Sample Evaluation Methods #1 (project was an apartment renovation for transitional housing):**

The success of this project will be based on the completion of the individual activities cited, the ability to provide the units for occupancy by the end of August 2014, and the savings in power/electric/utility bills for the Apartment Units. We will keep detailed records of the individual projects and the timetable/completion date of each, the dates of occupancy of each additional unit that is opened as a result of these projects, as well as the comparison of power/electric/utility bills after the upgrades as compared to the same month in previous years (so we can compare apples to apples for billing projections).

**Sample Evaluation Methods #2 (this sample is from a federal application):**

"Students Inspired" (SI) will offer all participants a minimum of 12-15 contact hours each week during the grant period. This time will be spent offering tutoring services, prevention classes, life skills, and enrichment activities so that program objectives/outcomes that align with NC State priorities can be achieved. Community Learning First (CLF) proposes that of participants, 75% will increase their math and reading grades by 5 points during the first academic year of participation. While a five point increase is the SMART objective outlined in Goals 1 and 2 under State Priority #1, staff will continue to work with individual students, teachers, and their parents to ensure that each participant achieves their own individualized learning goals in addition to program goals.

Goals 3 and 4 under State Priority #1 is focus on improving student scores from "not proficient" to "proficient" in reading and math assessments. The Program Director will adhere to best practice techniques as he/she trains program staff to deliver services and track student progress. Staff will use an appropriate and comprehensive data base such as Excel or Access to track both report card and standardized testing scores every 9 weeks. Each participant's academic performance will be evaluated by staff after 9 week data has been entered to determine if adequate progress is being made with the current implementation strategies or if tutoring/program changes need to be altered to increase performance levels.

The CLF is committed to ensuring that 100% of registered student have an "Individual Student Plan" and will be matched with an advocate within 30 days of program registration. Students will have the opportunity to select a mentor or will be assigned mentors provided through community partners such as Young People of Integrity.

Goal 5 aligns with NC State Standard #1 and addresses life skills and character education of all 3rd-12th grade participants. Through the implementation of interactive life skills, conflict resolution, prevention, and career readiness programming, it is the CLF's objective that a minimum of 80% of participants exhibit improved behavior. Evaluation measures for this program component include: school/program attendance records, formal discipline reports, teacher evaluations, and student/parent feedback. Pre and post-test will be used to evaluate the increase of knowledge in character education concepts introduced by community partners during program hours.

The CLF believes that it is reasonable to expect 75% of the 9th-12th grade students to engage in a minimum of 10 enrichment activities in year one. This objective: "to expose at-risk students to diverse opportunities to inspire growth on a personal level and become involved in the local community" falls under Goal #1 which aligns with State Priority #2. Because program strategies will be entertaining yet educational, the CLF expect fewer negative behavior incidences in the classroom/bus and a 75% increase in student interest to pursue career/college opportunities. Evaluation measures will be based on attendance records for program and extracurricular enrichment/educational activities, official school records, student/parent surveys, and the number of students who seek assistance to begin the career/college search and application process.

**Data Collection**

Family demographic information will be collected on all participants to demonstrate their true need for "Inspired Learning." Parents will authorize staff to secure official student/school records each nine-week grading period to be used as personal benchmarks for student progress.

Tutoring sessions with each participant will be tracked on a weekly basis by the Site Coordinator/Facilitator and records will be evaluated and recorded by the Program Director on a regular basis. Staff will create a student log sheet for each participant to note the following information during program hours: strengths/weaknesses in completing assignments, behavior, parent concerns, and/or the need to offer additional family support.

Nine-week progress reports, teacher evaluations, tutor evaluations, and parental evaluations will all be means of evaluating the effectiveness of this program and improvement of academic skills as previously stated. Knowledge of conflict resolution skills and prevention of negative youth behavior will be evaluated by means of pre- and post- tests as well as tracking of disciplinary action at school and the after-school program.

Parental involvement will be evaluated using attendance records for events and service hours logged with the staff. Project tracking of program components will be entered into an updated computer spreadsheet file. Required reports will be compiled by the Program Director and presented to the CLF advisory team for review before submission to 21st Century Community Learning Centers. Service quality of the program will be measured by 2 anonymous program evaluations: one administered to parents of students and a second evaluation completed by educators and administrators of participating schools. The Program Director will address all comments, needs, or concerns, and schedule a follow-up meeting with parents and teachers to ensure that appropriate and timely action was taken so that "Students Inspired" can create the positive change in the students, families, schools and community as a whole. Program data will then be compiled in a colorful and informative brochure and disseminated to the parents, schools, partners, stakeholders, and community. A pledge card will be included in this brochure to provide the community with a tool to offer donations so that the program can begin building a sustainable financial base.

## Potential Evaluation Methods

**Test**

Pre and Post Tests
Performance against control group

**Participation**

Attendance
Completion
Certificates
Follow-on tacking

**Data Collection**

Surveys
Questionnaires
Interviews
Checklists
Feedback forms
certificates

**Performance**

Grades
Graduation
Drop in recidivism
Job Placement
Permits, inspections,

**Financial Reports**

Cost to Budget
Cost per unit of service
On time on budget

**Subjective**

Journals
Testimonials
Observations
Photographs
Clippings

## Why do I have to list goals and objectives?

## 22. Why do I have to list goals and objectives?

In today's non-profit world, not all gifts are made with purely philanthropic intentions. In fact, many donors see gifts as investments. Donors who are well advised and experienced, be them individuals, foundations or corporations, are often looking for a Return On Investment (ROI). Donors want to know how their generosity has impacted a program, project, organization, community or population. It is important as a non-profit to be able to list goals and objectives, as well as have the ability to measure them so this data can be reported to the donor.

It is a good practice to have S.M.A.R.T. objectives for each goal. This means an objective that is Specific, Measureable, Attainable, Realistic and Timely.

**Sample Goal & Objective**

Goal (overall thing to be accomplished)

I want to lose 5% of my current body weight by August of this year.

Objectives (tasks that will help me achieve my goal)

- Begin walking 30 minutes a day 3 times a week by February
- Increase walking to 45 minutes a day 3 times a week by April
- Increase my intake of water to a minimum of 60 oz. daily immediately
- Reduce the number of deserts I eat to 3 times a week immediately
- Begin attending a 30-45 min. group exercise class weekly in May
- Increase the servings of vegetables I eat to 3 daily in February

These are just a few examples of potential objectives. Remember, the more objectives you list for any goal, the more you have to track for reporting purposes. Make sure that your objectives can be measured and that you have a time limit on them. Don't list a goal of 'lose weight by August of this year'. Be specific and say 'lose 5% of my current body weight by August of this year'. If you say 'lose weight', and you lose one pound, you technically achieved your goal. Donors are too savvy for these generalizations in today's world of giving.

## Question 23

What are overhead expenses?

## 23. What are overhead expenses?

Overhead expenses are all costs on an organizations income statement except for direct labor, direct materials, and direct expenses. Overhead expenses include such things as rent, repairs, maintenance, security, phone, utilities, travel, etc.

# Question 24

## What are fringe benefits?

**24. What are fringe benefits?**

Fringe benefits are any extra benefits supplementing an employee's salary and can vary from company to company. Some examples of fringe benefits are child care, dental insurance, 401K, flex spending, company cars, health insurance etc. Payments required to fund Social Security, unemployment compensation and workers' compensation programs, as required by law, do not count as fringe benefits.

# Question 25

## What are reimbursement grants?

## 25. What are reimbursement grants?

A reimbursement grant distributes funding to the recipient at benchmarks or certain intervals of a program/project instead of receiving all the money upfront. Most reimbursement grants come from state or federal agencies. Be sure to read grant guidelines and know if you are applying for a reimbursement grant. You will need to have money in the bank to cover the first several months of expenses because the reimbursement process can take several months to begin.

For example, I worked with an organization that received a reimbursement grant for their main program for over seven years. Each year, they had to have at least 3 months of funding in the bank to start the program (it was based on the local school system schedule). The organization submitted a progress report after month one. Despite timely reporting, lengthy review processes at the state level delayed reimbursements for up to three months. Organizations must have specific strategies in place to align program needs with available funds. Such strategies may include:

a) money in the bank to support monthly program expenses

b) a line of credit to cover monthly program costs until reimbursements are received

*During the economic crisis of 2009 there was a delay of six months before the first state reimbursement check was sent. So, be aware, there is no guarantee of payment at a particular time when you are dealing with reimbursements. Make sure your staff and board are aware of the potential issues with reimbursement grants and that you are able to operate successfully while you wait on those payments before you decide to apply for such funding.

# Question 26

## What are matching grants?

## 26. What are matching grants?

Individual donors, foundations and corporations often give money to nonprofits in the form of matching gifts or grants that require a match. Corporations also utilize matches in the form of employee matching gifts. An employee match means if an employee donates to a nonprofit, the employee's corporation will donate money to the same nonprofit according to a pre-determined match ratio.

Foundations and individual matching gifts are in the form of grants made directly to nonprofits, under the qualifying condition that the nonprofit raise a set quantity of money or in-kind contributions prior to the grant award being distributed. The benefit of foundation matching grants is that they provide greater incentive leverage when a nonprofit is fundraising from its constituency. If a foundation approves a dollar-for-dollar matching grant, donors know that their dollars will be doubled. On the other hand, foundations that give matching grants receive assurance of the nonprofit's desire and capacity to raise adequate funds.

# Question 27

Can a match be either dollars or in-kind?

**27. Can a match be dollars or can it be in-kind?**

Match requirements vary from foundation to foundation. Sometimes a match can be with in-kind contributions such as space, time, staff and materials. Other times a donor will require dollar-for-dollar matches. The details of match requirements can be found in the grant guidelines. If match requirements are not clearly defined in the guidelines, always reach out to the program office for clarification.

## Question 28

What does ‘in-kind’ mean?

## 28. What does 'in-kind' mean?

In-kind means that something is paid for or given through commodities, good, or services in lieu of money.

**Example 1:** A school is relocating and wants to donate chairs and tables to a nonprofit after-school program. The school does not require an exchange of money; they merely donate the furniture in-kind. They usually get a donation receipt from the nonprofit that can be used as a tax write-off for the value of the donation.

**Example 2:** A non-profit needs assistance upgrading software in a computer lab for client use, in addition to installing Malware and rebuilding a few computers. They would like to hire someone to complete this project, but there is no funding to make that happen. A local IT professional learns of the need and offers to do the work 'in-kind' (at no cost). This is a win-win for the non-profit. They get the work done at no cost, and they are able to report to donors the volunteer hours that went to the project. If this was a service that the volunteer usually charged for, the non-profit could provide a tax receipt for the value of the contribution which could be used as a tax write off.

# Question 29

## Should I list in-kind contributions on my grant budgets?

## 29. Should I list in-kind gifts on my grant budgets?

Yes. Donors like to see the level of community support your program/project has. One way to demonstrate this support is by listing in-kind contributions. Anything an organization would have had to pay for in order to complete a program or project, which is donated at no cost, is an in-kind contribution. These contributions can come in the form of volunteers/volunteerism, goods, services, space and/or materials. Be sure you keep a detailed record of volunteer hours and calculate the dollars saved for each project/program.

# Question 30

## Should my organization list in-kind contributions on their overall budget?

## 30. Should my organization list in-kind gifts on their overall budget?

Yes. Not only is it helpful to make donors aware of the organization's support, it is helpful to an organization so they can report to board, donors, members and staff. Organizations should have a realistic outlook on the support received from their community, and in what form that support is given (time, materials, volunteers, services etc.), because if the source of an in-kind gift was to cease to exist, how would the organization replace that in-kind contribution without affecting the overall budget?

For example: Let's say your organization is located in a building, along with several other non-profit groups, which is owned by a local school system. The school system only charges $50 rent per month. The rent is so low because they value your services to the community and the organization as a whole, and the building is not in high demand because of its' age. The county decides to tear down the dated building where your offices are located and you are forced to find a new space for your offices. How do you find a new location for $50 per month? How will your budget be able to handle the inevitable increase in your rent? This situation actually occurred with a non-profit in my area. They never kept good records of their in-kind contributions previously. Today, they keep track of ALL donations that come in the door so they can have a better plan for such situations in the future.

Never rely on a donor to make another gift, or source of in-kind contributions to continue their generosity. Have a backup plan.

***A smart non-profit is good at soliciting in-kind gifts. Part of the development process is looking over expenses and seeing where in-kind gifts can offset budget items. Once I served a shelter of homeless teenagers in New Orleans. We cut the cost of food in half through in kind gifts from restaurants and food vendors. (But we found out that even homeless kids were a bit skiddish at eating alligator!)***

***Over 28 years of non-profit work I have served or consulted with over 100 non-profits. We have always included in-kind gifts on our budgets for funders. It shows that we have exhausted every***

***means to help those we serve. And numerous funders have told me that they are impressed with our in-kind gift program. I think it will always work for you! – Alex Comfort, CFRE***

Question 31

What is supplemental information?

## 31. What is supplemental information?

Supplemental information is anything an organization might like to include with their grant proposal that was not requested/required in the application.

For example, if a donor requests an organizational chart or a copy of the recent 990, those would not be considered supplemental information. They would be considered required attachments. However, if they weren't requested by the funder, but an organization wanted to include a recent newsletter, a letter of support, or a DVD highlighting programs/projects.... Then those items would be considered supplemental materials/information.

Be sure to read the guidelines for each application carefully. Some donors will allow supplemental information, some will not, and some will ask organizations to include a multiple samples of the supplemental materials. It doesn't matter how badly you feel that an additional piece of material or marketing might help express your need or highlight a program.... If a donor clearly states that they do not accept supplemental items, do not send any.

## Question 32

## What is an organization chart?

## 32. What is an organizational chart?

An organizational chart (also referred to as org chart, organigram(me), or organogram is a diagram that shows the structure of an organization and the relationships and relative ranks of its various parts and positions/jobs.

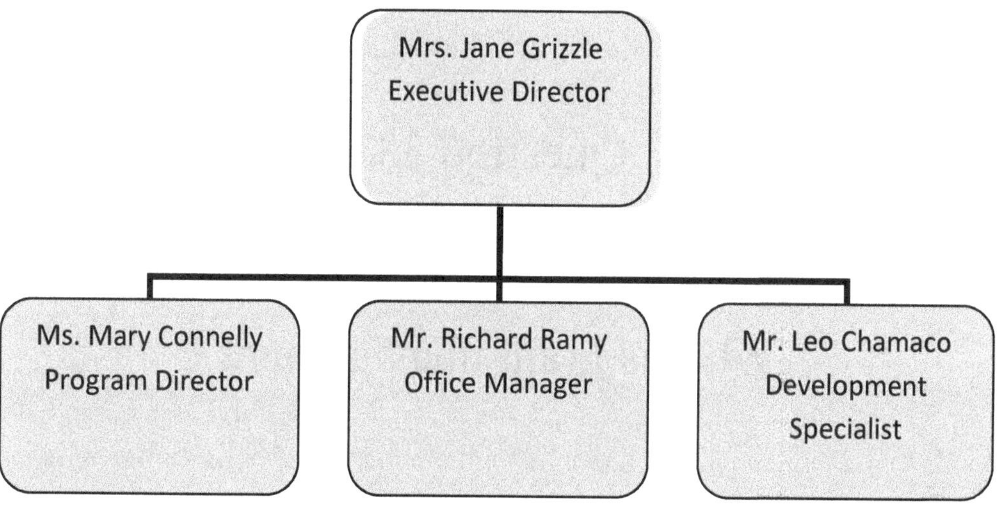

# Question 33

## What is grant management?

## 33. What is grant management?

Grant management is the process of keeping track of the data that needs to be reported to the donor as well as the actual reporting. Data can include benchmarks, goals, objectives, how funds were spent and so forth. Reporting can come in the form of site-visits, reports, interviews, submission of data, etc. Reporting can be monthly, quarterly, as benchmarks are met, biannually and annually. There is really no set time frame for reporting. These times will be determined by donors individually. Make sure you are clear on the amount of grant management required so you can make an informed decision on your organization's ability to fulfill the requirements.

# Question 34

## Who should manage our grants?

## 34. Who should manage our grants?

This answer will vary from organization to organization. However, the one answer which rings true in all situations is that the grant writer is NOT always the grant manger, and here is why.

If I am hired to write a grant for an organization, but I am not an employee of the organization, and I will not be working on the project once funds are received, it does not make sense for me to manage the grant. How could I possibly have the information needed to report, keep funders up-to-date, and make sure the project is on track with projected outcomes and so on.

Similarly, let's look at hospitals. If there is a 28 department hospital and each department is applying for grant funding from various sources, it is often the case that a hospital foundation may be submitting the applications, but not always managing the grants. The foundation may remind staff when reports are due. They may compile reporting data and help complete reports. But ultimately, the staff running the programs and keeping track of the data required for reporting, should be managing the grant.

In my professional experience as a grant writer, I never put my name on a grant (even if I have written it), unless I am the one responsible for the grant management. The reasons for this are:

- I should not be the one contacted by the funder when reporting questions arise.
- I should not be the one contacted when reports are not submitted.
- I am not working in the organization as an employee, or running the program/project the grant was written for, so I am unable to answer questions from a donor and will just end up referring them to the non-profit, which will frustrate the donor.
- If an organization is doing their due diligence with a donor and building a good relationship, the donor will expect to see a name they recognize on the grant application (be it a CEO, Executive Director, Program Director etc.) when questions arise about the application or project

## Question 35

## When do I report to the donor?

## 35. When do I report to the donor?

You report to the donor according to the terms outlined in the grant guidelines. Each donor will have a reporting timeline. Some are just once at the end of the grant, some don't require reporting at all, some need more frequency and some require site-visits and in-person reports on programs and projects. You will learn the pertinent information regarding reporting as you read the guidelines. If you are unclear on any of the reporting terms, you should clarify with the program officer *prior* to submitting your application.

Please note, it is NOT the donor's responsibility to remind grant recipients when reports are due. It is the organization's responsibility to remember and submit the reports on time. I recommend making notes on annual calendars several weeks before a grant report is due. This allows for time to collect any needed data, locate any missing data and complete reports in a timely manner.

Reporting on time is very important. There are donors out there who will not consider future funding if an organization fails to report according to the terms of the grant.

## Question 36

Do I have to report on how we spent the money?

**36. Do I have to report on how we spent the money?**

The answer to this question will be outlined in the grant guidelines. If you cannot find the answer, ask the program officer or person with whom you are building a relationship. Each organization will differ in their grant reporting requirements. It is important to maintain accurate book keeping. Donors may request a specific end-of-final budget report which outlines specific expenses. Other donors may request receipts to validate project expenses, while others may simply request a summary of how funds were expended.

## Can I go to the same donor every year?

## 37. Can I go to the same donor every year?

Donors are usually pretty clear in their guidelines about how often you can solicit them for a donation. Sometimes there are restrictions like once in a 12 month period, or once every two years, and sometimes there are no restrictions. Typically, if there are no restrictions, a request can be made during each grant cycle.

I have worked with donors who have multiple grant cycles annually, and many who have only one. It is your job as the grant writer to educate yourself on the guidelines of the organization, foundation or individual you hope to solicit for support.

I always say, "Building relationships is the most important part of grant writing." There is no exception here. If you build a solid relationship with the appropriate staff at a foundation/corporation, or with an individual donor, you should learn these types of answers during the relationships building process.

Be aware of other departments or individuals in your non-profit who have submitted applications to a potential donor as well. There is nothing more embarrassing than submitting more than one request for support to the same foundation during a grant cycle. Such oversights show lack of communication and organization on the part of the non-profit. If you ask permission to submit two different requests during the same cycle and a donor gives you permission, go ahead. But make sure you have permission beforehand.

Think before you ask. If you think a donor has lost some of the spark for your organization, maybe they have donor remorse or giving fatigue. Be sensitive to your donors and adjust your expectations accordingly.

# Question 38

## Should my board members give financial gifts?

## 38. Should my board members give financial gifts?

Always. Your board should give at 100%, every year ***at a leadership level.*** 'Leadership Level' might be vary by organization, but the level should be defined and clearly communicated to each potential board member. Non-profits should clearly set the expectations for giving by potential board members, prior to that person joining the board. You can do this through potential board member interviews or orientations, and/or written job descriptions reviewed one-on-one.

Additionally, it is important to have a process for board giving. A set campaign, schedule or calendar for asks, reminders, methods for making gifts and a deadline. If you want your board to give, you need to make it easy for them.

As you work in the world of grants, you will quickly see donors want to know if your board is giving, and at what level. This may come in the form of two questions.

1. What percentage of your board 'gives' to your organization. (They are asking what % of your board gives financially. They do not care about your boards' volunteerism, time, etc. They want to know who is giving dollars).

2. What percentage of your overall budget does your board giving comprise?

One of these two questions is asked on almost every grant I see. If your board doesn't support you financially, a donor may wonder why. You always want to be able to say you have 100% board giving.

> ***Absolutely! When someone agrees to join your Board, they become a leader of your nonprofit organization. And if the leaders don't personally support the organization, how do you expect anyone else in the community to give? More and more donors these days are savvy, and will expect to see 100% giving from your Board. You'll see more and more foundations asking for it, too. It's great when your Board members give their time and talent, and they need to give their treasure, too. – Sandy Rees, CFRE***

## Question 39

## Are grant deadlines flexible?

**39. Are grant deadlines flexible?**

Grant deadlines are not flexible. In fact, as more and more foundations move to online applications, the deadlines are automated. This means that at a certain time, on a certain day, the application process closes.

Read grant guidelines and talk with program officers to learn the deadlines prior to beginning the application process. This will help you set realistic expectations for work load and collaborations, as well as collecting data from those involved in the grant process.

It is better to submit early, than to take a chance on submitting late and losing the opportunity for consideration of a grant opportunity.

> ***No. No! Not even a little bit, except very rarely under extreme conditions determined by the funder. And the application must be complete. So, do not entrust the final packaging to a person who isn't detail oriented. For instance, I recently had a client ask a professional subordinate (not a grant proposal writer) to attach his 501(c)(3) proof of nonprofit status and then mail the application. She omitted the 501(c)(3) and the proposal was deemed incomplete.- Mark Goldstein, CFRE***

# Question 40

## How much should we ask for?

## 40. How much should we ask for?

Ask for what you need.

That being said, you should also do your research on the donor and build a relationship with them before you make your ask. You want to make sure you are asking for an amount that is within their typical gift range. You also want to make sure that they support the amount of the request you are submitting.

Also, keep in mind what portion of your overall need you are asking each funder to support. Are you asking them for 100% of your need? If you only need $2,500, asking for 100% might be a good strategy. If you need $1.2 million, it might not.

Make sure your asks align with your needs in a realistic way. A foundation that typically gives $5,000 gifts might not feel that their contribution would make a significant impact on a $1.2 million dollar project, unless you had secured a large portion of the funds prior to approaching them.

> ***When asking a foundation for a grant, read their guidelines! Often a funder will tell you exactly how much and when.***
>
> ***If the funder doesn't, you need to have a very good reason to ask for an amount far surpassing their average gift size. It is safest to stay within the range of their normal gifting levels. But if your organization truly needs more than has been funded in the past by this foundation, give them very good, concrete reasons why they should break their ceiling and plan for rejection on this criteria.***
>
> ***The best approach is to tell the truth and ask for a range of a gift and to explain how you came to the number (s). You can ask more than one funder for the amount and most funders ask to whom you are applying and for what amounts. Tell the truth. – Annie Fritschner, ACFRE***

---

---

***If you are applying for a government grant, there is usually a clear statement regarding how much can be requested. Foundations are frequently more hesitant to state an exact amount, and have often told me, "Ask for what you need." However, the best advice is to research the grant maker and learn what it typically gives to organizations or projects that most resemble your own. – Mark Goldstein, CFRE***

## Question 41

Do I have to get an official audit to apply for grants?

## 41. Do I have to get an official audit to apply for grants?

It depends on what the donor requires. Some will only require a 990 and year-end actuals, some will want a 990 and possibly a compilation report, and others will require a 990 and an official audit. Requirements should be in the grant guidelines.

> ***The bottom line is—not unless the funder specifically requires it. Even then, the grant maker may accept a financial statement if your organization has a relatively small budget, or may allow a less exacting (and less expensive) financial review. It seems to me that it is increasingly common for an audit to be mandatory, though, particularly for organizations that have budgets approaching or over $500,000. – Mark Goldstein, CFRE***

## Question 42

What’s the difference between a compilation report and an official audit?

## 42. What's the difference between a compilation report and an official audit?

*Certified public accountants can provide three basic levels of service in helping the board of directors gain assurance that their financial statements are more meaningful and reliable.*

*The first level of service is a compilation. The objective of a compilation engagement is to assist management in presenting their financial information in the form of financial statements, but does not provide any level of assurance on those statements. It is designed to only assist management in providing financial statements in the proper format and with all necessary disclosures.*

*The second level of service is a review. A review provides a limited level of assurance, which is less than an audit, but greater than a compilation. A review consists of applying certain analytical procedures to the financial information, but as mentioned is a lower level of service than an audit.*

*An audit is the highest level of service. An audit is designed to obtain reasonable assurance that the financial statements are free from material misstatement. It does not provide absolute assurance, but does give the board and other users a level of assurance that the financial statements are free from material misstatement.*

*There is a difference in cost to the organization for all three levels of service due the difference in time required to complete each type of engagement. The higher the level of service, the higher the cost to the board of directors. The decision of which level of service comes down to several factors, including specific requirements of the organization's bank, requirements of funding organizations, and the level of assurance that the board itself may require. – David Parsons CPA, a partner with DHW Certified Public Accountants & Consultants*

# Question 43

## What is a 990?

## 43. What is a 990?

Form 990 is the Internal Revenue Service (IRS) form entitled *Return of Organization Exempt from Income Tax*. This federal form must be filed annually by tax exempt organizations. However, some organizations such as churches are exempt from filing, and small organizations are allowed to file Form 990-EZ. The information provided on Form 990 is public information and is available on numerous websites.

*990's are a great way to do free grant and foundation research.

## Question 44

## What is a 990PF?

## 44. What is a 990PF?

The 990-PF is the IRS form for Private Foundations. This public document provides fiscal data for the foundation, names of trustees and officers, application information, and a complete grants list. The 990-PF is also a great source of research. It is a source to find complete grants lists for smaller and mid-sized foundations (who they funded). Larger foundations often issue annual reports, which provide descriptions of the grants awarded during the year for which the return is filed.

## Question 45

## Should I apply for every grant board members send me?

## 45. Should I apply for every grant board members send me?

You should not necessarily apply for every grant board members send you. First of all, you probably don't have time to be sitting behind your desk every day putting proposals together. A lot of board members are very well intentioned and think they are helping when they provide you with grant opportunities. What they may not realize is, you already have a 'plan' for your development department for the year, and it may or may not align with the proposal(s) they have presented to you.

Yes, if an amazing opportunity came up and a perfect grant came along, you would probably find time to work on that application. But, that is the exception, not the rule.

I remember working with a board member once that had a strong passion for a particular program. This board member was involved, participated, advocated for and financially supported the program. Additionally, this person was very proactive about finding grants that were in the same field as this program. I was constantly getting emails about grants I should be applying for. I was asked why we didn't apply for all of them and this board member got noticeably upset when I replied with the honest answers.

They did not understand that the organization had specific priorities for fundraising and this program was not really on that radar. They also didn't understand that spending 10 hours putting an application together for $5,000 to offer something that would cost $10,000, was not a good use of my time or the organization's resources.

It took a lot of talking, very nice emails and even other board members talking with this individual to get the point across. The help was appreciated, but there had to be some balance of understanding that just because I was a grant writer, I had many other hats to wear in the development department and could not spend all my time writing program grants.

You will have to learn the balance within your organization for these situations. The best tool you can have at your disposal is a **written fundraising plan**.

When you have a plan you can pull out and show to board members, you have a weapon that will help you disarm their insistence. As my friend Sandy Rees of Get Fully Funded says, "You can show a board member your fundraising plan and tell them that before you can add an additional item to it, you would first have to eliminate another part of the plan. This usually helps them step back and see that you have a full plate and you have a plan for success."

> ***Maybe. If the grant is a good fit for your nonprofit, then go for it. The problem is that the typical Board member doesn't understand grants and how to find the ones that are the right match for your nonprofit. When a Board member shares an opportunity with you, graciously thank them, then do your own research to determine if it's a good fit, and one that you should pursue. - Sandy Rees, CFRE***

# Question 46

## If I have money left over can I use it on whatever I want?

## 46. If I have money left over can I use it on whatever I want?

Absolutely not! If you have money left over from a grant, fabulous! It shows the donor that you have been fiscally responsible with the money they have awarded you. It shows that you have leveraged your resources, found sales, shopped around, solicited in-kind contributions and been a good steward of their gift.

As you work to build a relationship with the donor, you should be able to contact them and explain the situation. You can reach out when you see that you are going to have a surplus if it is in the middle of the project/program or at the end when you realize you have money left over. You should ask for permission to do one of several things:

- Transfer the left over funds to another line item where you could use those additional dollars. Sometime this will require you to fill out additional paperwork so the donor has a record of how the funds were spent and that they gave you their permission.

- Add a line item or two to the project that you realize you need/want/could benefit from thanks to the surplus

- Use the funds towards another project/program/general ops/overhead if that aligns with the funders priorities

This is NOT one of those times where you want to ask for forgiveness instead of permission. On occasion, a donor will require their money back. In that case, you don't want to have spent the money before getting permission to use it in a way that is not outlined in your grant proposal.

As always, build relationships with your donors and these conversations will go much more smoothly.

## Question 47

## Is there really enough money to go around?

## 47. Is there really enough money to go around?

Contrary to popular belief, there is enough money to go around. It may not come from the foundations you have always heard of or applied to, but it's out there. You might be surprised to know that there is a great deal of grant funding that never gets awarded because no one ever applies to receive it.

I have on numerous occasions been called by foundation program officer asking if I knew of a non-profit that might apply for a grant cycle, because there were no applicants. I have seen state and federal grant dollars never claimed and state dollars returned to the government because they were not applied for locally. Rest assured there is money out there.

> ***As a fundraising consultant who directs a lot of capital campaigns, one of the most amusing things about talking to a prospective client is discussing whether or not it is a good time to do a campaign. Normally the client lists a lot of reasons it is a bad idea to do one. But almost all those reasons will still be there in two years. Therefore, since it is always a bad time to do a campaign, you might as well go ahead.***
>
> ***Donors never give you their last dollar. Period. And non-profit leaders are not thinking about the whole world, really, but what is right for them. The question is really, "Is there enough money for us to do what we need to do?" Gail Perry, a consultant from Raleigh, NC, tells people that there is always enough money to do what is needed <u>in your current data base!</u> She believes, if we ask the right way, and with the right case explanation, there will be enough. Even if she is being overly optimistic, I believe we should start by being confident that there will be enough money to accomplish your need.***
>
> ***In the capital campaign world, we always accomplish a feasibility study to determine a reasonable probability of success. About 20% of the studies I have done suggest using a lower goal for the actual campaign. For grants it is important to be realistic with the client. If your research doesn't give you a lot of promise, be honest with your client.***

---

*Let's put it this way – there is plenty of money out there, but your case and cause has to be compelling in order to be funded.*

*In my area we recently saw an example that gives one caution, however. A non-profit announced a $24 million dollar campaign, and the local universities had never gone that high. Some early major gifts came in tied to having sight preparation done quickly, and within a year the rest of the giving had not matched the pace. The result: one of our major regional children's non-profits went bankrupt. Poor planning, optimistic, unrealistic thinking, and a bit of non-profit arrogance did it in. Well, and the recession as well. (I'll also toss in that the group said they didn't need a consultant as part of the process.) My point is that bad planning and unrealistic projections can threaten a non-profit.*

*So, yes, there is enough money for everyone, but non-profits are also businesses. Many points of view must be considered, and experienced people should be consulted. If the dream is supported by enthusiastic donors and grantors who have the capacity to support the dream, it can be accomplished. But capacity must be merged with need, value, and the proper leadership. – Alex Comfort, CFRE*

---

*You bet! Over $300 billion dollars are given to charity in the US alone each year. If every person who gives simply gave 1% more, think of the amount of money that would suddenly flow into nonprofits everywhere! Worrying about enough money indicates a poverty or "lack" mentality. Instead, focus on the possibility of what could happen if your donors decided to increase their giving. Then do all you can to make it happen by inspiring them with stories of your organization in action.- Sandy Rees, CFRE*

---

## Question 48

## Why don’t donors give away more money if there is a need?

## 48. Why don't donors give away more money if there is a need?

Foundations are only required to 'give away' 5% of their assets annually. Some donors choose to make exceptions and make additional charitable contributions based on need, passion or special RFPs. But the *required* amount remains 5%. In order for grant cycles to be available on an on-going basis, donors have to pace themselves and set up realistic giving amounts. If they give away all the money they have in one year, or in one grant cycle, there won't be an additional pot of money to continue giving from in the future.

The concept of growing an endowment applies to foundations. If there is a pot of money that earns interest, a portion of that interest should/could be drawn down for charitable giving. The principle of the fund should stay intact, and a portion of the interest reinvested so the base always grows. As foundation dollars grow, giving amounts follow suit and allow for greater impact over time.

I truly believe foundations want to give more. Foundations exist to 'do good' some would say. When foundations can do more good, I've seen them find ways to leverage their funds, make matches to other donors, give in-kind when applicable and support through door opening and networking when giving more financially is not an option.

Question 49

What is the difference between project and program grants?

## 49. What is the difference between project and program grants?

Programs are long term and projects are short term. Donors are often inclined to fund projects because they have an end date and the donor knows that the organization will not need additional funding for that in the future.

Organizations looking for program grants have an easier time finding funding when the program is new, growing, expanding to other areas, encompassing a new demographic etc. Securing funding for a program that is not growing, even when it provides for a great need, is not the easiest thing in the world. It can be done, and some programs have a limit to their capacity and always will… you need to know the type of program you are looking to represent in a grant before you begin looking for the dollars.

# Question 50

## Can I find money for salaries?

**50. Can I find money for salaries?**

Yes. You can find money for most needs, if you have a good plan, project or program to 'sell' to the donor, if you match your needs with their priorities, and you tell a compelling story. I have yet to find a non-profit need that there was not funding to support. You have to do the leg work to make sure you are building relationships, researching foundations and *their* priorities, and have all your ducks in a row before reaching out to talk with foundations.

Additionally, you must to submit a quality proposal. Don't assume because you have a great relationship with a donor that you can slack on the proposal. Do everything you do, to the best of your ability, and then ask for a second set of eyes to review your work. That is when you will know you have done all you can and you should feel good about your effort.

**In closing…**

For those of you who have had the opportunity to participate in a ***Funding for Good*** workshop you know that Mandy often asks participants to share their "Ah-hah" moment. Those are the moments that the light bulb flashes on and new or developing grant writers can say, "NOW I get this!" This book was designed to provide readers with 50 of those "Ah-hah" moments by breaking down complex grant writing components into simple segments and straightforward examples.

It is important to remember that while this book serves as a wonderful guide for aspiring grant writers, the opinions shared represent the experiences of the professionals in the field who contributed to this publication.

Every grant writer must learn to develop relationships with donors, evaluate what information is being requested in a proposal, and respond to those questions their own concise yet personal writing style.

We sincerely hope that **Grant Writing | What The Pros Know: 50 Things I Wish I Had Known Before Writing My First Grant,** has equipped each of you with tools you need to become a confident grant writer and that you are now ready to help the projects and communities you believe in most find *funding for good.*

-Marie Palacios, Non-Profit Director and Professional Grant Writer

## CONTRIBUTORS

Beth S. Brodovsky
President, Iris Creative Group, Inc.
Communications Builds Community
iriscreative.com

Pamela Grow, Founder
Simple Development Systems
pamelagrow.com

Alex Comfort, CFRE.
President, Mountain Non-Profit Solutions, LLC
mn-ps.com

David Parsons, CPA
Partner with DHW Certified Public
Accountants & Consultants
dhw.net

Annie Fritschner, ACFRE
Fundraising Coach+Trainer+Speaker
annie@anniefritschner.com

Sandy Rees, CFRE
Founder and Chief Encouragement Officer
Get Fully Funded
getfullyfunded.com
sandy@getfullyfunded.com

Mark Goldstein, CFRE
CEO, Communication Mark
communicationmark.com
mark@communicationmark.com

Lynne M. Wester
Principal and Founder, Donor Relations Guru LLC
lynne@donorrelationsguru.com
donorrelationsguru.com